www.moshimonsters.com

HERE BE MONSTERS

SUNBIRD

Published by Ladybird Books Ltd 2010
A Penguin Company
Penguin Books Ltd, 80 Strand, London, WC2R 0RL, UK
Penguin Group (USA) Inc., 375 Hudson Street, New York 10014, USA
Penguin Books Australia Ltd, Camberwell Road, Camberwell, Victoria 2124,
Australia (A division of Pearson Australia Group Pty Ltd)
Canada, India, New Zealand, South Africa

Written by Steve Cleverley
Illustrations by Vincent Bechet and Trevor White
Sunbird is a trade mark of Ladybird Books Ltd

www.ladybird.com

ISBN: 978-1-40939-035-0
008 - 8 9 10
Printed in China

THE MOSHLING COLLECTOR'S GUIDE

Contents

Burnie 18   Humphrey 20   Jeepers 22   ShiShi 24

DJ Quack 30   Peppy 32   Prof. Purplex 34   Tiki 36

Blurp 42   Cali 44   Fumble 46   Stanley 48

Dipsy 54   Flumpy 56   Honey 58   IGGY 60

Doris 66   Gurgle 68   Pooky 70   Snookums 72

Chop Chop 78   General Fuzuki 80   Sooki-Yaki 82   Shelby 84

7

Greetings, Fellow Moshling Hunters!

Yours truly

Buster Bumblechops, Moshling expert extraordinaire at your service.

If you're looking for Moshlings, then you've come to the right place. This handy field guide is jam-packed with everything you need to know about the teeny-weeny critters. And I should know, because it was written by yours truly. Yep, that's me!

What I don't know about Moshlings isn't worth remembering. In fact . . . erm, oh Barbecued Bubblefish! I forgot what I was going to say!

Thing is, I've been chasing these small wonders since I was knee-high to Mr Snoodle. And that's a mighty long time.

Buster aged 3 1/4

My first traps weren't always very successful . . .

ut how did I become obsessed by Moshlings?
isten up . . .

It all started many moons ago when my great
ncle, the legendary Moshlingologist, Doctor
Furbert Snufflepeeps, vanished while looking
for Big Bad Bill in the Gombala Gombala
Jungle. The only things the search party
found were his notes and hunting hat,
crumpled up and covered in gooey blue
star seeds. **Sniff!**

The second I read those ucky notes and
plopped that gloopy hat on my head, I knew
exactly what I had to do: take a shower!
After that, I decided to spend my days
(and nights) tracking and studying Moshlings.
The rest is history.

Finding Fishies in
Potion Ocean . . .

My crazy
adventures have
taken me all
over (and under)
the wacky world of Moshi, from the
soggy depths of Potion Ocean to
the fluffy pink clouds high above
Mount Sillimanjaro. Along the way,
I've wrestled General Fuzuki on the
shores of Lake Neon Soup, hidden
from Ecto in Collywobbles Castle
and chased Cutie Pie across Candy
Canyon. Or did she chase me?
I can't quite remember . . .

I've even fallen off a runaway SkyPony (painful, cos I landed on my moshiscope), sat on Hansel (a crummy accident) and eaten a fiery frazzledragon (tasted just like chicken).

And let's not talk about the time I single-handedly fought off a gang of Cheeky Chimps because, um, I didn't. The naughty scamps pelted me with custard pies and ran off with my spinoculars. **Splat!**

Writing this handy guide

Even though I have been in all kinds of pickles, I still adore Moshlings . . . I've even written poems about them . . .

Some are friendly, some are shy.
Some are scary, some can fly.
Some like sipping lukewarm coffee
and brushing their teeth with toffee.
Some like doing the splits and
chewing marmalade with bits.

And believe it or not, some like eating Moshling hunters!

It's true. Just ask my trusty sidekick, Snuffy Hookums. Actually, don't bother - she's missing, presumed consumed by a mysterious tribe of unknown Moshlings near the lava lake of Mount KrakkaBlowa. If you bump into her on your travels, do say hello from me. Much obliged.

Tiki loves my Great Uncle's hat!

As you can tell, Moshling hunting is not all fun and games. Well, okay, it is. But it takes a special kind of monster to tame these itty-bitty beasties. Think you can handle it? Keep this book with you at all times, and at least you'll know what to expect next time you come face-to-face with Ecto the fancy Banshee!

Good hunting!

Buster Bumblechops

Buster Bumblechops
The Ultimate Moshling Collector

Contact me at:
buster@moshimonsters.com

Collecting Moshlings

Howdy doody, eager beavers! Are you ready to start nabbin' yourselves a few Moshlings? Good, cos when it comes to roundin' up the playful little scamps, your old pal Buster is an expert.

Of course, some of my rootin' tootin' trapping techniques are far too risky for all you whippersnappers out there. And I wouldn't want you vanishing into thin air like my poor ol' great uncle!

So, how do you get your mitts on a Moshling without risking your neck? All you need are seeds! They're the sure-fire way to attract the teeny-weeny critters. So quit scratching your noodle and check out my seed-tastic tips. They're sure to grow on you!

STAR BLOSSOM

SNAP APPLE

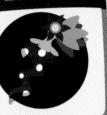

OT SILLY PEPPERS

As any budding collector knows, Moshlings are attracted to flowers — and seeds make flowers. Just hightail it over to

www.moshimonsters.com

and buy yourself some seeds. If you're lucky enough to be a Moshi Member you can skedaddle on over to the Port area and buy extra-special seeds like Crazy Daisies and Snap Apples to attract rarer Moshlings.

MOON ORCHID

n total there are eight
eird and wonderful seed
arieties. Plant them in the
hree plots in your garden
and watch 'em grow. Sounds
easy, huh? Well, sometimes
t is, but different blooms
attract different Moshlings,
so you need to get your
combinations just right.
You dig?

DRAGON FRUIT

LOVE BERRIE

MAGIC BEANS

CRAZY DAISY

If you're looking to snag something Ultra Rare, you'll need to make sure your flowers are the right colour, too. Hot diggity, talk about fussy! If you don't get lucky straight away, relax. A birdie boffin called the Cluekoo will swoop in with a few helpful hints. Next time you crack a combination, why not share it with your friends?

Keeping your Moshlings

Collecting Moshlings isn't quite as easy-peasy-gooberry-squeezy as ol' Buster makes it look. But once you get the hang of it you'll be swamped with little pets, so you'll need somewhere to keep 'em.

After all, who wants squillions of kooky characters scurrying, fluttering and waddling around their crib? Exactly! And I wouldn't recommend stuffing them in your pockets or keeping them under your hat. That's why the Moshling Zoo is so cool.

Ideal for serious collectors, you can keep as many Moshlings as you like in here. Each time you complete a set of four, your Moshlings pen gets a funky makeover. The lucky critters even get their very own theme houses to hang out in. Mmm, home sweet home!

ZOO

14

alking of home,
you're a Moshi Member,
ou can keep up to six
oshlings in your room
t any time. Simply move
hem between your zoo
nd house by clicking
the zoo signpost.
witcheroodle-doo! You can
en set your Moshlings
ee if they don't tickle
ur pickle.

Baby Tumteedums love a cuddle!

By now you're probably
wondering where I stash all
the Moshlings I've collected
over the years. No, I
don't keep them in my
tent. I don't even send
them to a zoo or put
them in the backyard at
Bumblechops Manor.

Truth is, they are free to wander
around my secret Moshling ranch,
a supersize sanctuary hidden right
next to . . . oops, well, slap my
head and call me silly! I almost
forgot it's a secret. Search all
you like, you'll never find it. And
believe me, many of my rivals
have tried!

Moshling Ranch
17 Secret Street,
Moshi World

Beasties

With a name like Beasties, you would be forgiven for thinking these Moshlings were wild and ferocious. Thankfully most of 'em are harmless, though I've had a few tricksy run-ins with them in my time. Jeepers will even let you tickle its tummy if you hand over a few cans of swoonafish.

Even Ultra Rare Fiery Frazzledragons can be kept as pets — so long as they don't get hiccups and burn the house down. Perhaps it would be best to kick-start your Beastie collection with a Sneezing Panda. These snuffly channel surfers are happy to go anywhere there's a big screen and remote control.

Or maybe you should plant some seeds for a Snoring Hicko. They are pretty easy to attract and spend most of their time catching Zs. But so would you if you gulped lazy daisy moonshine all day.

Most Moshlingologists believe Beasties are direct descendants of Sillysauruses, which means they are slightly related to Dinos. But don't tell them that. Who wants a snarly ol' lizard for a granddaddy?

Oh yes, I almost forgot. All Beasties can recite the alphabet backwards.

Ynnuf, huh!

zyxwvuts rqponmlk jihgfedcba

Burnie
the Fiery Frazzledragon

Personality: combustible, dangerous, cheeky

Too hot to handle!

ULTRA RARE

Burnie

Flaming hiccups!

Other Beasties:

Humphrey the Snoring Hickopotumus	✓
Jeepers the Snuggly Tiger Cub	✓
ShiShi the Sneezing Panda	✓

If you can stand the heat, you might find a few fiery Frazzledragons fluttering around Mount CharChar, on the volcanic island of Emberooze.

These cheeky flying beasties get into all kinds of sizzly mayhem, especially if they've been guzzling gasoline. It's their favourite drink but it gives them terrible flaming hiccups. Stand back or you might get toasted! (I've been lightly barbecued a few times, but nothing too serious.) Some time ago I discovered ancient scribblings in a cave by the Lava Lakes. My translator, Dr Unwin Babble, thinks they prove Frazzledragons were once employed by Super Moshis to heat up cauldrons of dew stew and chargrill silly sausages.

Hiccup!

Paw print

Habitat

Likes: ☺
Ash-flavoured hotcakes and the Fizzbangs' new single.

Dislikes: ☹
Fire extinguishers and round tables.

Code to catch Burnie:

SNAP APPLE	SNAP APPLE	CRAZY DAISY
RED	RED	BLUE

Humphrey
the Snoring Hickopotumus

Personality: happy-go-lucky, snoozy, bumpkinly

Yee-hah! Quit lollygagging around and say howdy to the good ol' Moshlings that love digging, sowing, milking and mowing. If they're not busy working the ranch, Snoring Hickos enjoy grabbing forty winks under the shade of a wacky windmill. Trouble is, forty winks often turns into forty hours and that's a mighty long time when you're supposed to be mixing lazy daisy moonshine.

I've been lucky enough to visit several Hicko ranches, and nothing beats watching the sun go down after a rollicking barn dance and a few slugs of Hicko firewater.

'Urp!

Habitat

Snoring Hickos live and work on the ranches scattered across Skedaddle Prairie down Whoop 'n' Holler Valley.

Likes: ☺
Pickin' the banjo and chewing enchanted corn.

Dislikes: ☹
Concrete and the smell of manure in the morning.

Awake, for once!

Catching some ZZZZZZZS

Humphrey

Code to catch Humphrey:

CRAZY DAISY **ANY** + HOT SILLY PEPPERS **ANY** + MAGIC BEANS **ANY**

21

Jeepers
the Snuggly Tiger Cub

Personality: bashful, soppy, cuddly

RARE

Jeepers

Oops, I pressed 'zoom'!

Pesky critter
got its claws
on my notes!

Code to catch Jeepers:

LOVE BERRIES

ANY

+

SNAP APPLE

BLUE

+

CRAZY DAISY

RED

Even though their camouflage is useless, it's pretty difficult for a normal monster to spot a Snuggly Tiger Cub because they seldom stray beyond the lush foliage of the Barmy Swami Jungle.

These adorable Moshlings really have earned their stripes. That's because they spend ages painting them on using inka-inka juice, squeezed from rare thumpkin seeds. Sadly the jungle is green, not yellow and stripy, so an expert like me has no problem spotting them.

I once disguised myself as a Snuggly to infiltrate their tribe. Sadly it rained and the paint washed off, leaving me looking very silly, licking my paws and scratching for fleas. When they're not slopping hopeless camouflage around, Snuggly Tiger Cubs love sharpening their claws and licking old swoonafish cans.

Habitat

Other Beasties:

Paw print

Likes: ☺
Glam rock and having their tummies scratched.

Dislikes: ☹
Water pistols and flea collars.

ShiShi

the Sneezing Panda

Personality: friendly, brainy, snoozy

ShiShi

ULTRA RARE

Code to catch ShiShi:

DRAGON FRUIT

RED

+

HOT SILLY PEPPERS

YELLOW

+

CRAZY DAISY

BLACK

Originally from Gogglebox Gulch, these snuffly channel surfers will live anywhere as long as there is a big screen, comfy chair and remote control.

Habitat

Aah-choo!
These eyelash-fluttering Moshlings are obsessed with watching Monstrovision, but it makes them sneeze. Lots. My research suggests they might be allergic to all those itty-bitty pixels. Or maybe it's the wamwoo shoots they scoff by the bucket-load. I'm not really sure because I've never had a proper conversation with one. I've tried, but when they're not glued to the screen, Sneezing Pandas are usually fiddling with magical eye drops or scrunching up extra-soft tissues. Next time I spot one, I might just switch off whatever it is they are watching and observe what happens.

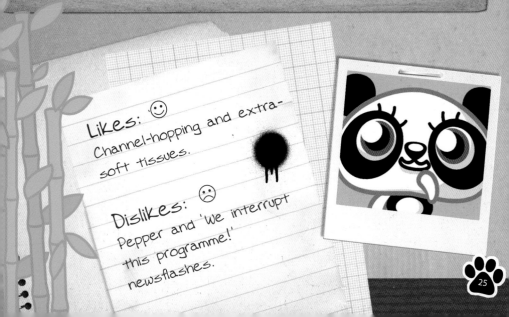

Likes: ☺
Channel-hopping and extra-soft tissues.

Dislikes: ☹
Pepper and 'we interrupt this programme!' newsflashes.

When it comes to jotting down stories about rounding up Beasties, I could scribble away for ages. So I will!

After all, they are such a mixed bunch: from Humphrey and ShiShi to Burnie and Jeepers. And tracking them down never fails to lead to a rip-roaring adventure.

The first Beastie I ever came across was Burnie. I spotted the flame-spewing fella through the high-powered moshiscope aboard my research ship, *Windigo II*, whilst circling the volcanic island of Emberooze.

It was flip-flapping around Mount CharChar collecting lava lumps. But I couldn't get too close cos that place is hotter than a bear's backside in a pepper patch.

Anyhow, I finally enticed the sizzly little firestarter into the crow's nest with a flask of gasoline and a few ashcakes. At first he was jumpier than spit on a hot pan, but he soon relaxed and spilt the beans – he was carrying a tin of vindaloo-flavoured ones for his lunch!

Over a tongue-scorching snack, he told me all
about his fellow Beastie Moshlings. Me?
I couldn't do much yakking because the
beans were burning my mouth and
everything I thaid thounded
really thilly!

Worst of all, when I tried to trap
him in my net he let out an almighty burp and
set fire to my sails. Vwoomp! Thankfully, I was
rescued from the blaze by a gaggle of Valley Mermaids riding
Songful Seahorses, just as my beloved boat slipped beneath
the waves.

Phew-ee!

From that day on I vowed to beware of Beasties,
even the ones that can't breathe fire. And it's a
good thing I did because I almost came a
cropper thanks to a cub called Jeepers and
a Hicko by the name of Humphrey . . .
but that's a whole 'nuther story!

PS: According to my Fishie friends,
the *Windigo II* is still in one piece
at the bottom of Potion Ocean!
Maybe y'all can salvage some
equipment for me next time
you're in the area? Thanks!

Birdies

Squawk! Apart from beaks, wings and feathers, Birdie Moshlings have got little in common. Stunt Penguins can't even fly! (Well, they can, but piloting old-fashioned biplanes doesn't really count.) In fact, the only time Birdies get together is for the annual Birdie Bash, a crazy rave hosted by Disco Duckies over on the TakiTaki Islands.

But things used to be very different. Oodles of years ago, all four Birdie species lived together in Fluttertown, an ancient tree-village that is now submerged, deep beneath Lake Inferior.

Birdie life was much the same as it is today: Pilfering Toucans would steal sunglasses from Disco Duckies (who in those days were known as Classical Quackers), Stunt Penguins would torment Sabre-toothed Splatterpillars and Owls of Wiseness would occasionally look up from their books to tut.

According to legend, the Birdies went their separate ways after the devastating Moshi custard flood of 99999.5. These days, although they don't really mix, Birdies can be found flapping, waddling, swooping and sliding all over the world of Moshi, from Wobbly Woods to Lush Lagoon. Plant the right seeds and you might see one sooner than you think.

Look, up in the sky. . .

DJ Quack
the Disco Duckie

Personality: funky, big-headed, completely quackers

DJ Quack

Disco Duckies live on the Taki Taki Islands in the middle of Lake Neon Soup. Well, it's more of a pond really, but don't tell them that.

Habitat

You can tell by the way they waddle that these groovy little quackers were born to boogie. Matter of fact, I had to wear purple legwarmers and blow on a funky whistle to bag my first Disco Duckie. And what a jive-quacking critter it was!

When they're not flapping around mirrorballs and dipping their beaks in glittery gloop, these music-mad Moshlings are busy busting out new dance moves and slicking back their feathers with orange sauce. If you ever meet one in a dark alley, be sure to duck – they can't see a thing with those shades on.

Likes: ☺
Quacking in time to the beat and moonwalking.

Dislikes: ☹
Silence and getting peanut butter stuck in their beaks.

Get down to the underground disco!

Code to catch DJ Quack:

DRAGON FRUIT		MOON ORCHID		STAR BLOSSOM
ANY	+	ANY	+	ANY

Peppy

 # 071

the Stunt Penguin

Personality: reckless, rebellious, wheely obsessive

Peppy

RARE

Code to catch Peppy:

MOON
ORCHID
ANY

+

MAGIC
BEANS
YELLOW

+

MOON
ORCHID
RED

32

Despite being rubbish at riding bikes (their feet don't reach the pedals), these cool little Moshlings are obsessed by anything with two or more wheels. That's why they slide along on their tummies making vroom-vroom noises and revving the air with their stumpy wings. One dotty daredevil even tried to climb aboard my MoshiMobile, but couldn't find the keys.

As well as their need for speed, Stunt Penguins love scoffing pilchard popsicles by the bucket-load. That's lucky for me because I always keep a few of these yuckity treats in my backpack. Here, pengy wengy!

Stunt Penguins can be found on the frosty Pop Glacier, a wintry wonderland near Potion Ocean. When lost, they usually head for the nearest fridge.

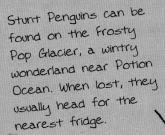

Habitat

Likes: ☺
Engine oil and buckets of fish heads.

Dislikes: ☹
Beards and being poked in the belly button.

Peekaboo!

Prof. Purplex
the Owl of Wiseness

Personality: bookish, well-read, well-fed

Prof. Purplex

Rockin' + readin'

RARE

Code to catch Prof. Purplex:

 DRAGON FRUIT — **ANY**

+

LOVE BERRIES — **PINK**

+

MOON ORCHID — **YELLOW**

Owls of Wiseness can be found high in the trees of Wobbly Woods. They don't like being disturbed and only leave the branches if they run out of reading/nibbling material.

Habitat

Banned by every library and bookshop in the land, Owls of Wiseness are brainier than big brain pies with extra brain sprinkles. Able to digest an entire encyclopedia in ten seconds, these birdie boffins have a real appetite for knowledge – literally, because they will scoff any book they see. That's why I always use my great uncle's old notebook as a trap – it's mighty interesting and covered in icky-sticky owl-grippy gloop. Now who's the brainy one?

Likes: ☺
Books, newspapers and plinky toy pianos.

Dislikes: ☹
Stupidity and bowler hats.

Meditating on his wiseness

Tiki
the Pilfering Toucan

Personality: mischievous, pesky, chirpy

Scouting for shiny things

Colourful but crafty, Pilfering Toucans can't resist 'borrowing' things from other Moshlings, especially salty gobstoppers. I say borrow, but what I really mean is steal, because these thieving flappers are the naughtiest pirates on the planet.

You won't believe how quickly they can swipe your pocket money and stash it in their beaks. Maybe it's because Pilfering Toucans once sailed the seventy seas alongside some of the meanest monsters in history. One thing is for sure, catching 'em is harder than knitting gravy. I always use a pile of gold coins and a big ol' net. Least I did – till they were stolen.

Darn!

Habitat

Pilfering Toucans nest high in the palm trees near Lush Lagoon. Look up and you'll see coconut-hair hammocks filled with all kinds of loot.

Likes: ☺
Playing the squeezebox and drinking punch.

Dislikes: ☹
Barbecues and catapults

Watch out, Tiki is lost!

Tiki

RARE

Code to catch Tiki:

STAR BLOSSOM	+	LOVE BERRIES	+	LOVE BERRIES
ANY		PINK		RED

Peppy: Monstro City's Greatest Stunt Rider!

Chasing Tiki keeps
me on my toes!

Fishies

Even if you've never studied fishtory, you don't need to be a brain sturgeon to know what links Fishies together. Give up? It's big, blue and really wobbly. No, not the cashier at Yukea, I'm talking about the ocean. So slip on your flippers, suck on your snorkel and listen up!

These sub-aquatic Moshlings can't get enough of the beautiful briny sea — or anything else that's remotely wet. But that doesn't stop 'em ploppin' above the surface whenever it tickles their fins.

I've seen Acrobatic SeaStars somersaulting along Main Street and Valley Mermaids eating seaweed sandwiches by Firebreath Fountain. (Then again, I had been drinking wobble-ade in the Aargh Bar that night.)

Speaking of mermaids, the enormous Sea Mall deep beneath Potion Ocean is their fave new hangout. But you're just as likely to see a Songful Seahorse bobbing along the aisles whilst a Batty Bubblefish shops for ink refills.

As you can tell, Fishies get along famously. Well, the ones on the following pages do — because although I've identified just four 'offishal' species, I'm pretty sure there are plenty more fish in the sea. So, watch this space — failing that, go jump in a lake. Glug!

Blurp
the Batty Bubblefish

 # 043

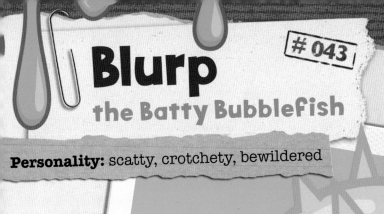

Personality: scatty, crotchety, bewildered

Watch out, wormy!

Blurp

Icky gloop – yuck!

Code to catch Blurp:

MOON ORCHID
ANY

+

LOVE BERRIES
ANY

+

LOVE BERRIES
PINK

All puffed-up with nowhere to blow, Batty Bubblefish spend most days swimming around in circles holding their breath. In fact, these marine Moshlings have got such terrible memories they can't remember what it is they're supposed to have forgotten. A bit like me!

Never upset one, as they can splurt out gallons of multi-coloured gloop – something I learnt the hard way when I tried to examine one with my giant underwater fish spatula. It took me months to get that stuff outta my whiskers. Still, at least I won't forget the incident – I've got a nasty stain on my swimsuit to remind me!

Stand back, he's ready to blow!

Habitat

Batty Bubblefish live in the foamy waters beneath Fruit Falls. Hang around and you might see one leap out of the water, blow a raspberry and plop back under.

Likes: ☺
Old flip-flops and . . . erm, can't remember.

Dislikes: ☹
Fish fingers and swallowing water.

Cali
the Valley Mermaid

Personality: ditzy, sassy, caffeineated

RARE

Cali

STARFISHBUCKS COFFEE

Habitat

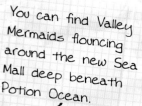

You can find Valley Mermaids flouncing around the new Sea Mall deep beneath Potion Ocean.

To use Valley Mermaid lingo, 'Like, wow . . . there's something totally fishy going on here.' Confused? Me too. I need to consult my mermaid translation book every time I hear one of these ditzy fishies speak. Maybe I'm getting old. What-ever!

When they're not freaking out over the latest koi band or knocking back cappuccinos at the local Starfishbucks, these hip little cuties love hooking up fellow Moshlings. In fact, their hearts flash whenever they sense romance. Lucky for me they are usually too busy yacking to notice this old timer scribbling notes.

Duh!

Likes: ☺
Seaweed sandwiches and chilling out in crates of ice.

Dislikes: ☹
The Boogie Woogie Bluegill Boys and rusty anchors.

What did the sea say to the mermaid?
Nothing, it just waved!

Code to catch Cali:

MAGIC BEANS **ANY** + LOVE BERRIES **YELLOW** + LOVE BERRIES **BLUE**

Fumble

the Acrobatic SeaStar

Personality: gnarly, fearless, full of beans

Gimme five! Or four? Or how about three? Because when they're not cartwheeling along the seabed performing death-defying stunts, Acrobatic SeaStars spend most days gluing their pointy bits back on. They're a bit accident-prone, you see. Thing is, they can't resist showing-off, even if it means tumbling face-first into a pile of poisonous seagrass. Now that's gotta hurt!

A while back, I got mixed up in a crazy pile-up when I was snorkelling in Potion Ocean; a troupe of SeaStars bungeed off a coral formation straight onto my head. Lucky I still had my trusty hat on.

Habitat

These energetic Moshlings live amongst the coral ree-of Bleurgh Lagoon but ofte gather on the beach to body surf.

Likes: ☺
Removing bandages and thrash metal.

Dislikes: ☹
Safety nets and outboard motors.

RARE

Fumble

Code to catch Fumble:

STAR BLOSSOM **ANY** + LOVE BERRIES **YELLOW** + MAGIC BEANS **YELLOW**

Stanley #018
the Songful SeaHorse

What's the difference between a fish and a piano? You can't tuna fish!

Personality: flamboyant, tactless, ear-splittingly noisy

Splish, splash! Stanley taking a bath!

Stanley

Putting out fires!

Songful SeaHorses are not very good swimmers so they usually bob around the shallow waters of Reggae Reef. Failing that, look in the bath.

Habitat

Although they are very cute, Songful SeaHorses can be incredibly annoying. That's because they can't stop whistling awful show tunes really loudly. Each ear-splitting ditty is usually accompanied by a barrage of bubbles and a silly dance. My research suggests they are trying to attract other SeaHorses, but I've been unable to stand the racket long enough to confirm this. Even earmuffs are useless. That's why I've invented a special squishy snout plug to muffle their trumpety blasts. All I need now is a volunteer to sneak up and plop it in. Any takers?

Likes: ☺
Kazoo concertos and sea oats.

Dislikes: ☹
Bubble bath and serious opera.

Code to catch Stanley:

DRAGON FRUIT ANY + LOVE BERRIES ANY + LOVE BERRIES ANY

Where are the Fishies?

Stanley

Blurp

Cali

Fumble

51

Fluffies

If you're looking for cuddles, you've come to the right place! Fluffies are soft, squishy and impossibly cute. I still wouldn't recommend snuggling one until you are an expert collector — some of 'em bite and some have thundery tempers.

Take IGGY. This Ultra Rare Pixel-Munching Snaffler just loves scoffing pointy arrows (cursors, I think you keyboard-tappers call 'em). Anyhow, little IGGY (short for "I'm Gonna Get Ya") is quite a handful and often pops up out of nowhere, vanishing before you can say 'control', 'alt' or even 'delete'.

Far more relaxed are Honey and Flumpy. These snugglesome Fluffies are friendly as can be. Which is more than can be said for Dipsy. Don't get me wrong, this weeny wisp of mysterious fluff is mostly angelic. Trouble is, she tends to pour with rain the second she is upset.

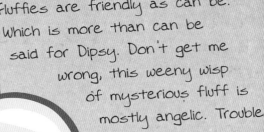

Although Fluffies can be found all over the land of Moshi, I don't think they are of this world. I reckon they originated from deep within the Squishy Dream Dimension, an ultra-squashy place that only appears if you close your eyes and cuddle your pillow. Awww, cute!

Dipsy
the Dinky Dreamcloud

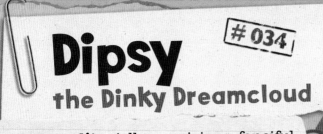

034

Personality: jolly, capricious, fanciful

Dipsy

Habitat

Dinky Dreamclouds are native to Meringue Meadow, an area surrounded by towering vanilla pod trees and wild candiflop.

Likes: ☺
Doing the splits and marmalade with bits.

Dislikes: ☹
Modern dance and clumpy shoes.

Dinky Dreamclouds dream of becoming Ginormous Dreamclouds, but they are far too teeny for such an important job. That's why they flutter and flap about all day, making cute noises and admiring their eyelashes. Don't get them angry, or they might rain on you – something I discovered when I tried to poke one with my telescopic Moshling prod. The fluffy little creature hovered over my head for the rest of the expedition, bucketing down on me every time I tried to shoo it away. Worst of all, I'd forgotten my umbrella.

Aah-choo!

Other Fluffies:

Flumpy the Pluff

Honey the Funny Bunny ✓

IGGY (or "I'm Gonna Get Ya") ✓

✓

The Pixel-Munching Snaffler

Code to catch Dipsy:

MOON ORCHID **ANY** + LOVE BERRIES **ANY** + MOON ORCHID **YELLOW**

Flumpy
the Pluff

Personality: cheerful, carefree, big-hearted

Habitat

Pluffs originally come from the Cotton Clump plantations, but you'll often see them strolling around town, smiling at the world.

Many monsters think Pluffs are the most chilled-out Moshlings of all. And it's hard to disagree when you see them strolling through the Cotton Clump plantations, arms dangling, grinning as if they haven't a care in the world. If you want to chillax, you can't beat hanging out with a gang of Pluffs.

I've enjoyed many a sunny afternoon stretched out on my deckchair 'researching' these friendly Fluffies. They don't even mind when I take photos and ask them to sign my postcards. Wish you were here? It's a tough job, but someone's gotta do it.

Likes: ☺
Rubber gloves and furniture polish.

Dislikes: ☹
Clutter and the smell of damp.

RARE Flumpy

What's white and fluffy?
Flumpy.
What's blue and fluffy?
Flumpy holding its breath!

Code to catch Flumpy:

STAR BLOSSOM
ANY

+

MAGIC BEANS
RED

+

MOON ORCHID
BLACK

57

Honey #057
the Funny Bunny

Personality: outgoing, natty, chatty

Honey

RARE

Code to catch Honey:

MAGIC BEANS — ANY

+

LOVE BERRIES — YELLOW

+

SNAP APPLE — BLUE

You might expect these rabbity Moshlings to live in basic burrows, but most of them own incredibly modern hutches in Pawberry Fields.

Habitat

What's Honey's favourite game? Hopscotch!

Dedicated followers of fashion, Funny Bunnies are the best-dressed Moshlings in town. Yes, I know that's hard to believe looking at my stylish outfit, but it's true. I'm pretty sure they think I'm hip. Well, they always chuckle and point when they see me.
  If they're not busy texting jokes to their friends, these incredibly cute furballs can be found yacking about carrot cake, clothes and fur straighteners. Talking of straightening, all Funny Bunnies have one floppy ear. I'm convinced this is caused by listening to silly ringtones all day.

Likes: ☺
Sniggering at silly jokes and ironing flowers (especially naffodils).

Dislikes: ☹
Orange sauce and lukewarm nincomsoup.

IGGY
the Pixel-Munching Snaffler

100

Personality: unpredictable, hyper, bouncy

Aargh! Curse those pesky cursors!
  These pixel-scoffing Moshlings look innocent enough, but the second they spot a pointy arrow, it's history. I've spoken to a few keyboard-tapping geeks and they believe Snafflers find computer cursors really annoying – like flies flittering around their heads. But seeing as they can't swat them (they've got no arms, let alone rolled-up newspapers) they gobble them up. It's not just arrows though: my precious hat has been munched from my head on several occasions. It must taste funny, because the Snafflers always spit it straight out.

Yuck!

Habitat

You might occasionally spot a Pixel-Munching Snaffler trapped in a hedge, but they usually whoosh in from mysterious portals in cyberspace, called Aargates.

Likes: ☺
Power surges and tickly pickles.

Dislikes: ☹
Delete keys and nifty mouse-operators.

t many people know
s, but IGGY stands
r 'I'm Gonna Get Ya!'

ULTRA RARE

IGGY

Spit out my cursor!

Code to catch IGGY:

MOON ORCHID		CRAZY DAISY		CRAZY DAISY
BLACK	+	**PURPLE**	+	**PURPLE**

Diary

Cute and cuddly? Maybe, but there's no time for snuggles when you are searching for Fluffies. I've had some of my greatest adventures trapping these little softies . . .

This afternoon I managed to snaffle the Ultra Rare IGGY - and I'm not even a computer geek! I stuck an arrow-shaped bit of card to a glueberry bush and waited for the greedy gobbler to pounce. The second it took a bite outta my pretend cursor, it was stuck. Lemme tell ya, that pesky varmint was madder than a mule chewing bumblebees. Gotcha!

It must be my lucky week Fluffie-wise, because yesterday I collected several Funny Bunnies using a newfangled contraption called a 'mobile phone'. I just sent a text telling them where to meet and herded them straight into the party prairie on my Moshling ranch. They were too busy nattering, texting and nibbling my home-baked carrot cake to notice.

As for Dinky Dreamclouds, to avoid getting drenched I find it's always best to entice them down to ground level with marmalade and wild candiflop. I also pack an umbrella, just to be on the safe side.

62

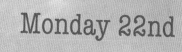

But how about Pluffs? Well, there's no need to go chasing these easy-going Moshlings. They are happy to do whatever I tell 'em. Why, I'm resting my tired tootsies on a snoozing Pluff as I write this very page.

Yes, siree, Pluffs and Buster go together like grits and gravy. "Hey Flumpy, don't forget to massage this here little piggy that went to market."

Dinos

Do you fancy having a totally Jurassic lark?
Then why not bag yourself a few Dinos?
These prehistoric Moshlings have been
roaming the world of Moshi since the
year dot. Maybe even longer.

Hatched from itty-bitty eggs, they are
said to be descendants of a race of
giant dinos (known as 'Doyathinkysaurus)
but seem to have shrunk somewhere
along the line. Either that or everything
else just got a whole lot bigger.

As well as thick skin and a ridiculous fear
of rubber spears and chest hair,
Dinos have incredibly small brains.
That's not to say they are
dim, they are just a bit . . .erm,
slow on the uptake. Take
your average Performing

Nappasaurus, for example, dumb as a
heap of fossilized fungus flakes, it will
happily eat its own body weight in squishy
marshmallows before waking up to discover
its pillow is missing.

One more thing to remember: Dinos are
petrified of enormous asteroids. Not that
you see many of those round these
parts. Oh yes, and they love chocolate
mice. But it's probably best to stick with
seeds if you wanna nab yourself a few.

Doris
the Rummaging Plotamus

 # 040

Personality: gossipy, fluffle-loving, nosy

Doris

Other Dinos:

Gurgle the Performing Flappasaurus

Pooky the Potty Pipsqueak

Snookums the Baby Tumteedum

Rummaging Plotamuses live anywhere there are fluffles to be found (usually under trees), so Friendly-Tree Woods is a popular hangout.

Habitat

Unlike regular Plotamuses, Rummaging Plotamuses are obsessed with digging for fluffles – valuable toadstools that smell of liquorice. These gentle Moshlings then knit the fluffles into nests and hibernate in them for much of the year. I was the first Moshi to tame a Rummaging Plotamus. I even got mine to knit me a fluffle jumper. Thing is, it smelt so good I couldn't resist munching it.

When they're not burrowing, knitting or snoozing, Plotamuses love gardening (well, digging up dirt) and gossiping about celebrities. And that's what makes them ideal pets – as long as you're not famous.

You dig?

Likes: ☺
Manicures and reading gossip columns.

Dislikes: ☹
Quiet Moshlings and tall garden fences.

Code to catch Doris:

| MOON ORCHID | | MOON ORCHID | | MOON ORCHID |
| ANY | + | ANY | + | BLACK |

Gurgle

 # 083

the Performing Flappasaurus

Personality: prestidigitatory, fame-hungry, showy-offy

Gurgle

ULTRA RARE

Habitat

Likes: ☺
Pulling rabbits out of hats and toasted marshmallows.

Dislikes: ☹
Bad audiences and soggy matches.

68

What do you call a
Dino with no eyes?
Do-you-think-he-saw-us?

Roll up, roll up! Performing Flappasauruses are the entertaining little Moshlings that always have a trick up their wings. The tricks usually go wrong, but I find it's best to applaud, because these jolly dinos are very sensitive. When a magic routine goes really badly I've seen them burst into tears and toast their props with a burst of fiery breath. But hey, that's showbiz! Examining Flappasauruses is pretty easy because they're massive show-offs. They'll even pose for photos and give interviews if you tell them you work for *The Daily Growl*.

Ta-daa!

Unlike most Moshlings, Performing Flappasauruses enjoy living in the full glare of the Cadabra Flash, a gleaming light formation near the Crazy Canyons.

Ta-daa!

Code to catch Gurgle:

DRAGON FRUIT **RED** + LOVE BERRIES **PURPLE** + MAGIC BEANS **YELLOW**

Pooky
the Potty Pipsqueak

 # 050

Personality: playful, imaginative, silly

Pooky

Code to catch Pooky:

MOON ORCHID
ANY

+

MAGIC BEANS
ANY

+

MAGIC BEANS
PURPLE

How do Moshi Monsters like their eggs?
...rri-fried!

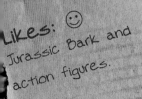

Likes: ☺
Jurassic Bark and action figures.

Dislikes: ☹
Washing their paws for dinner and sausage skins.

With their cracked eggshell helmets, Potty Pipsqueaks are often mistaken for newly hatched Moshlings. They claim to wear this strange headgear to protect themselves from Killer Canaries. But why would tropical birdies want to attack? Simple, the eggshells belong to them. Potty Pipsqueaks steal them so they can pretend to be racing drivers and spacemen. I know it sounds crazy, but I've witnessed an attack. I was hiding in a gooberry bush watching two Potties playing, when a flock of angry birdies swooped. Looking back, I'm glad my camera jammed. It wasn't a pretty sight. Broken eggshells everywhere.

Habitat

Potty Pipsqueaks come from Make-Believe Valley, but I've found them playing in cardboard boxes disguised as spaceships, fire engines and tanks.

Snookums
the Baby Tumteedum #010

Personality: timid, long in the tooth, trusting

Snookums

Habitat

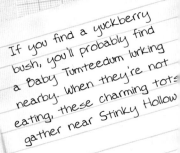

If you find a yuckberry bush, you'll probably find a Baby Tumteedum lurking nearby. When they're not eating, these charming tots gather near Stinky Hollow

Perhaps the cutest Moshlings of all, Baby Tumteedums are sweet little demi-dinos that just want to be loved. Hatched from mysterious marzipan eggs, these wide-eyed critters are always looking for someone (or something) to look after them. And that's strange, because they age in reverse, so babies are actually hundreds of years old. It's just a shame they're not very chatty, as I'd love to find out if these old timers know anything about my great uncle's disappearance. Unfortunately they're always too busy scoffing yuckberries and boiled eggs dipped in vinegar.

Likes: ☺ Boiled cabbage and carpet slippers.

Dislikes: ☹ Loud music and toenail clippings.

Must remember to buy more vinegar . . . .

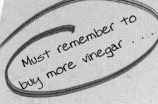

Code to catch Snookums:

STAR BLOSSOM ANY + STAR BLOSSOM ANY + STAR BLOSSOM ANY

My Photos

A bumper crop of yuckberries had the Baby Tumteedums flocking to my garden this year!

Hmpfh. I got a bit of a dunking just after this photo was taken . . . that pesky Pooky.

Ninjas

Legend has it that somewhere over the rainbow, in the Land of the Surprising Sun, Ninja Moshlings once lived together, training, meditating and chopping planks of wood in half with their heads. These days, Ninjas aren't half as silly — they are ten times worse.

Hi-yaaa!

Most of them wear bandanas, hoods or helmets because they think it's good for their stealth. But the truth is, you can spot a Ninja a mile off — even Caped Assassins can't help popping up when they are supposed to be hiding. And Cheeky Chimps can't resist playing pranks and shouting 'boo!'

s for Warrior Wombats, well, they might
e Ultra Rare but these noble Moshlings
pend most days snoozing. Slapstick
ortoises? They are too busy having
nishaps to do much at all.

Apart from a love of sushi and badly
dubbed kung-fu movies, the one thing that
inks Ninjas together, even today, is their
ability to speak ancient Moshlingese —
a strange language that even I struggle
to get my tongue around.

Chop Chop
the Cheeky Chimp

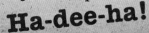

Monkeying aroun

Personality: ninjarish, naughty, impish

As well as being part-time ninjas, Cheeky Chimps are full-time jokers. They leave a telltale trail of whoopee cushions, banana skins and stink bombs wherever they roam. In fact, these playful primates don't know when to stop. And that can be pretty funny, unless the joke's on me.

Over the years I've been pelted with gooberries, squirted by plastic flowers and even had ink smeared around my spinoculars. Watch out, or you could end up with a face-full of custard pie and a rubber chicken in your soup.

Ha-dee-ha!

Habitat

Most Cheeky Chimps swing through the vines of Sniggerton Wood, but some prefer hiding in closets before jumping out and shouting 'Boo!'

Likes: ☺
Tying shoelaces together and flicking ears.

Dislikes: ☹
Political talk shows and runny porridge.

What did the banana say to the monkey? Nothing. Bananas don't talk.

Chop Chop

Code to catch Chop Chop:

 +  +

General Fuzuki
the Warrior Wombat
082

Personality: serious, mysterious, reliable

General Fuzuki

Catchin' some ZZZZZZs

Knock! Knock!
Who's there?
Warrior
Warrior who?
Warrior you been all my life?

ULTRA RARE

Code to catch General Fuzuki:

HOT SILLY PEPPERS

RED

+

LOVE BERRIES

YELLOW

+

STAR BLOSSOM

PURPLE

I heard a rumour that Warrior Wombats were once used to guard Rox and other precious things. But that's not because these furry little Moshlings are fearless. It's because legend has it they don't need any sleep. Or do they? My research shows that their 'open eyes' are actually titchy cake tins welded to their hats. This allows them to take forty winks on the sly. Napping on the job? Now that's naughty. Still, at least it helps me study the rare little sleepyheads. I just sneak up with my snore-o-meter and get busy.

Warrior Wombats live in the sub-zero wastelands of ChillyBot State Park, a mysterious place where darkness never falls. Pack your shades!

Likes: ☺
Shiny objects and comfy cushions.

Dislikes: ☹
Alarm clocks and bits of food in beards.

Sooki-Yaki
the Caped Assassin
047

Personality: stealthy, wide-eyed 'n' bushy-tailed, evanescent

Sooki-Yaki

If cars run on petrol and cookers run on gas, what do caped assassins run on?

Code to catch Sooki - Yaki:

HOT SILLY PEPPERS

ANY

+

MAGIC BEANS

ANY

+

MAGIC BEANS

RED

Most Caped Assassin sightings have been reported near East Grumble. If you're lucky, you might see one suddenly appear halfway up a drainpipe. I have and it scared me silly!

Habitat

Now you see them, now you still see them! And that's because Caped Assassins are not as good at sneaking around as they think they are. Don't laugh, because these agile little Moshlings possess the ability to vanish and reappear in an instant. They don't even register on my Moshling detector.

The problem is, they can't control their power and always pop up when they shouldn't. I should know, because the first Caped Assassin I ever saw appeared right in front of me just as it was about to . . . er, well I never found out. It disappeared again.

Likes: ☺
Gadgets and knitting.

Dislikes: ☹
Itchy collars and slippery roof tiles.

Shelby

the Slapstick Tortoise

Personality: bonkers, clumsy, gormless

Shelby

What was the tortoise doing on the motorway? About fifty millimetres an hour!

Slapstick Tortoises are highly-trained Moshlings. It's just a shame whoever trained them was dumb as a stump. The only thing they're good at is messing up their moves and tumbling on to their wobbly shells. They can't even tie their own bandanas. And that's bad because they're supposed to be ninjas. If only they stopped watching silly kung-fu movies, they wouldn't be so useless.

I encountered my first Slapstick Tortoise whilst collecting shrillberries. In fact, I nearly trod on it because it was flailing around belly-side up.

Hi-yaaa!

Shelby, age 5 months

Likes: ☺
Brushing their teeth with toffee and buffing up their shells.

Dislikes: ☹
Laying belly-side up and jogging.

These gormless Moshlings hibernate under the boardwalk at Groan Bay but often gather to compare (and then mess up) new fighting moves at the Wailing Wharf.

Habitat

Code to catch Shelby:

DRAGON FRUIT — ANY + MAGIC BEANS — ANY + DRAGON FRUIT — BLACK

Where are the Ninjas?

GIFT SHOP

Chop Chop

Shelby

Sooki-Yaki

General
Fuzuki

FACTORY

Gift
Island

Worldies

Introducing Worldies, the wacky Moshlings that bear an uncanny resemblance to landmarks you might just have seen somewhere before. Totally monu-mental, these walking, talking critters were once lifeless objects that sat hidden around the world of Moshi looking bored and neglected.

The poor things had been around for so long, most monsters didn't pay them much attention, unless they decided to pose beside one for touristy photos. In fact, the only creatures that visited Worldies on a regular basis were the birds - don't ask why, just use your imagination. Plop!

But then one day, as if by magic, the Worldies
suddenly came to life. It was as if they had been
sleeping the whole time. Exactly how it happened
is still a mystery, but I think it may have been
caused by a blast of OoperDuper energy from
deep inside the Umba Thunk Mines. Or maybe the
Worldies just got bored with standing around all day.

Since waking from their slumber, Worldies have
become extremely popular, especially amongst
snap-happy sightseers and Moshling collectors.
So read on and get planting . . .

Liberty
the Happy Statue

RARE

Personality: brash, confident, cheery

Liberty

Habitat

Likes: ☺
Big apples and star-spangled sweeties.

Dislikes: ☹
Rust and flash photography.

Happy Statues live on Divinity Island but rumour has it they were shipped over from a mysterious land called Prance.

Pretty!

With a lipsmackin' ice cream in one hand and a never-ending wish list in the other, Happy Statues believe in having fun, playing games and making wishes. They even wear magical crowns that glow every time they think up a new wish. It's not that these cheerful Moshlings are greedy, they just adore dreaming about yummy treats, cool clothes and twinkly trinkets. You go, girl!

Happy Statues are amongst my favourite Moshlings because they welcomed me with open arms (and lots of apple pie) when I first landed on Divinity Island. I wish all Moshlings were that friendly.

Liberty wishes it was raining jelly beans!

Liberty was designed by Moshing Collector Chaowzee in a design-a-Moshling competition!

Other Worldies:

Mini Ben the Teeny Tick Tock	✓
Cleo the Pretty Pyramid	✓
Rocky the Baby Blockhead	✓

Code to catch Liberty:

LOVE BERRIES
BLACK

+

LOVE BERRIES
RED

+

LOVE BERRIES
ANY

Mini Ben
the Teeny TickTock

Personality: posh, dandified, eccentric

Mini Ben

ULTRA RARE

Teeny TickTocks can often be spotted bonging around the foggy banks near Westmonster Abbey.

Habitat

Around the world

'CLONG!' Don't be alarmed, Teeny TickTocks are the noisy Moshlings who love chiming on the hour, every hour. I always stuff my socks in my ears when I'm tracking them down. Why? Because I once startled a sleeping TickTock and the bonging nearly burst my eardrums. Ouch!

When they're not swaying to and fro, making their bells go bong, these terribly old-fashioned chaps enjoy waxing their bushy moustaches, nibbling cucumber sandwiches and asking everyone the time. Well have you ever tried looking at a clock that's stuck on top of your head? It's harder than you think!

Likes: ☺
fish and chips with hot, sweet tea.

Dislikes: ☹
Earmuffs and cuckoos.

How can you tell if Mini Ben is hungry? He'll go back for seconds!

Code to catch Mini Ben:

SNAP APPLE	SNAP APPLE	SNAP APPLE
BLACK	BLACK	BLACK

Cleo
the Pretty Pyramid

080

Personality: sunny, smiley, fun-loving

What did one Pr
Pyramid ask th
How's your mum

Most experts (but not me!) thought Pretty Pyramids were extinct, until a fierce sandstorm blew away a huge desert dune to reveal the lost valley where they live and play. Needless to say, yours truly was already on the scene following a tip-off. Thank goodness for that storm – I'd forgotten my shovel.

Apart from bathing in milk, munching on grapes and making massive sandcastles, these friendly Moshlings spend their days searching for lost treasure and painting funny squiggles on walls. They also love riddles, precious stones (especially Rox) and anything made of gold.

Likes: ☺
Their mummies and shiny, twinkly things.

Dislikes: ☹
Sandy suntan lotion and archaeologists.

Code to catch Cleo:

SNAP APPLE **YELLOW** + CRAZY DAISY **BLUE** + CRAZY DAISY **PINK**

Habitat

Most Pretty Pyramids live in the Lost Valley of iSissi, near the banks of the River Smile.

Cleo

ULTRA RARE

Rocky

the Baby Blockhead

Personality: rugged, thoughtful, brave

Rocky

Code to catch Rocky:

HOT SILLY PEPPERS — **ANY**

LOVE BERRIES — **ANY**

CRAZY DAISY — **PINK**

at is a Baby
ckhead's favourite music?
ck and roll!

They might be stony-faced and a little dense, but Baby Blockheads can be really helpful. That's because these super-heavyweights are very, very strong – hardly surprising as they're made from solid rock! They even sweat liquid concrete when lifting heavy objects – bad news for me, as I once stood in a puddle of Blockhead sweat for a little too long and got stuck. Thank Moshi I only lost my boots!

Speaking of getting into trouble, Blockheads don't know their own strength and can sometimes break things, especially fingers when they're shaking hands. Crr-unch! Best to just say hi.

Lets ROCK!!

Likes: ☺
Rock music and fluffy rabbits.

Dislikes: ☹
weeds and jackhammers.

Habitat

These incredible bulks live on Beaster Island where they often sit for hours, staring out to sea.

"Living thingies that look just like mini monster-made structures? You've gotta be kidding!" Yep, those were my exact words when I first heard about this bizarre band of Moshlings.

But then I stumbled across Rocky. Quite literally because the stony-faced statuette was hiding in the grass. Yow! Scared me silly and darn near broke my toe.

I soon discovered Blockheads are slower than treacle, so the next time I spotted one I dropped my hat on it and tried to pick it up. Big mistake, as these incredible bulks are amazingly heavy. Tore my hat, my undies and even a muscle in my back. If you haven't got the right seeds, I recommend you bend your knees when lifting one or buy a mighty big crane!

Much easier to catch are Happy Statues. I sometimes entice them with apple pie and twinkly trinkets, but they are usually happy to be nabbed by a living legend (that's me!) and simply follow me back home.

If only Teeny TickTocks
were as trusting. These
upper-crust ding-dongers
don't take kindly to
collectors. Matter of fact,
they usually try poking
intruders away with their
umbrellas and bonging their
bells. Best way to trap 'em is
to change the time on their clocks
when they are sleeping. Confuses 'em
rotten. What time is it?
It's collection time!

As for Pretty Pyramids, I find the best
way to catch 'em is to lay out a trail of
buckets and spades. They just can't resist
making sandcastles. Failing that, fill a bath
with milk and you might get lucky.

Foodies

Feeling peckish? Then you'd best grab yourself a snack, because reading about Foodies is sure to get your tummy rumbling. These edible Moshlings are just about the strangest critters I ever did see. And let me tell you, they really are delicious.

Nobody knows exactly how Foodies came into existence, let alone who decorates them with sprinkles and icing sugar. Whoever it is, I'd sure like to lick their spoon!

Scoff all you like, but I've managed to grab a bite, lick, chomp and nibble of every Foodie out there. And that's no mean feat, because these scrummy things are either Rare or Ultra Rare. If you want to inhale their sugary aroma, you'll need to get your seed combos just right.
Mmm . . . sweet!

f you're lickin' ya lips in anticipation,
on't bother. It takes years of
experience to get close enough to take
a bite out of a Foodie. And some of 'em
ain't exactly friendly! I've had quite a few
run-ins with Psycho Gingerboys (the meanest
Moshlings of all) and even Ringy Thingies are not
so sweet when you're chasing them across the
boiling oil swamps of Greasy Geezer - unless you
fancy a face-full of sticky sprinkles. You do?
Then read on . . .

Coolio
the Magical Sparklepop

Coolio

the Magical Sparklepop

052

Personality: deliquescent, cool, upbeat

What do Sparklepops sing on birthdays? Freeze a jolly good fellow!

I know it sounds a trifle absurd, but these tubby Moshlings are enchanted. Whenever they need to chill, glittery sparks zing around their slurpy swirls accompanied by jingly-jangly nursery rhymes. This happens quite a lot because Magical Sparklepops go all gloopy if it gets too hot. That's why I always try to observe them when the sun is coming out. If the weather won't play ball, I hide behind a snowdrift and give 'em a quick blast with my hairdryer. It's sparkletastic! But what's with the funny waddle? Well, you try walking wearing a wafery tub.

Habitat

Coolio, 6 months

Magical Sparklepops prefer chilly areas - for obvious reasons. That's why you'll find them around Knickerbocker Nook in the Frozen Dessert Desert.

Likes: ☺
Whackcurrant sauce and crushed nuts.

Dislikes: ☹
Too much sun and big tongues.

102

Twinkle, twinkle little Sparklepop!

Coolio

RARE

Code to catch Coolio:

STAR BLOSSOM	LOVE BERRIES	SNAP APPLE
ANY	**BLACK**	**PINK**

Cutie Pie
the Wheelie YumYum

091

Personality: zoomtastic, chummy, quick-witted

Cutie Pie

Sprinkle-tastic!

ULTRA RARE

Code to catch Cutie Pie:

DRAGON FRUIT

BLUE

+

STAR BLOSSOM

PINK

+

CRAZY DAISY

PURPLE

Check out the wheels! These scrumptilicious Moshlings move like lightning. But so would you, if you had turbo-charged sprinkles and a woowoo-ing cherry on your head. Wheelie YumYums are often forced to flee from hungry predators, leaving spongy crumbs in their wake. Follow the trail and you might find one filling up with a few gallons of super-sweet cocoa. I find the only way to keep up with these zippy foodies is to get on my rocket-powered roller skates and give chase. I've never caught one, but those crumbs are delicious!

A cakey aroma often wafts across Ramekin Plain, so I think CutiePie Canyon (where Wheelie YumYums are rumoured to live) could be located nearby.

Habitat

Sprinkles

Likes: ☺
Steaming hot drinks and fancy napkins.

Dislikes: ☹
Silly aprons and chocolate chip traffic cops.

Hansel
the Psycho Gingerboy

Personality: disobedient, loutish, rascally

Hansel

RARE

Sweet tunes!

Code to catch Hansel:

DRAGON FRUIT		MAGIC BEANS		MOON ORCHID
ANY	+	BLACK	+	BLACK

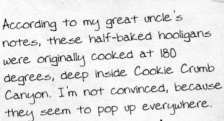

According to my great uncle's notes, these half-baked hooligans were originally cooked at 180 degrees, deep inside Cookie Crumb Canyon. I'm not convinced, because they seem to pop up everywhere.

Yikes!

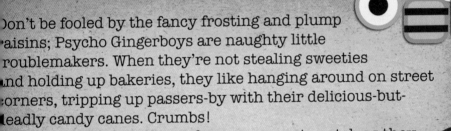

Don't be fooled by the fancy frosting and plump raisins; Psycho Gingerboys are naughty little troublemakers. When they're not stealing sweeties and holding up bakeries, they like hanging around on street corners, tripping up passers-by with their delicious-but-deadly candy canes. Crumbs!

Thankfully, Psycho Gingerboys are easy to catch as they can't help dropping yummy crumbs wherever they go. I hear a bunch of 'em are out to get me, because I accidentally squashed one of their pals. Looks like I'll have to fill my water pistol with milk to soften up the biscuity bullies.

Likes: ☺
Twirling liquorice lassos and bathing in custard.

Dislikes: ☹
Cheesy puffs and pecking pigeons.

Oddie # 088
the Sweet Ringy Thingy

Personality: sweet, boisterous, cautious

Oddie

Oddie's not that glazed look in his eyes again . . . .

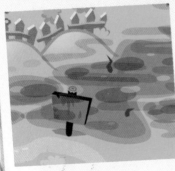

Habitat

ULTRA RARE

I believe Sweet Ringy Thingies are formed and fried in the boiling oil swamps near Greasy Geezer. Exactly who decorates them remains a mystery.

With their doughy bodies and gloopy icing, Sweet Ringy Thingies look exceedingly delicious – and they are! That's why these squishy hoops are always on the move. Everyone wants a piece, especially Moshling collectors who haven't eaten for days. It's a good thing Ringy Thingies can blast attackers with volleys of hundreds and thousands, otherwise they'd be extinct. I've still got a few pink bits stuck in my eyebrows following a recent attack.

If you're wondering how a bunch of sticky doughnutters ever became living, breathing Moshlings, don't. I'm still trying to get to the bottom of it myself.

Likes: ☺
Words beginning with 'O' and hot oil.

Dislikes: ☹
Purple sprouting broccoli and coffee (especially being dunked in it).

Code to catch Oddie:

STAR BLOSSOM **PURPLE** + STAR BLOSSOM **BLACK** + STAR BLOSSOM **YELLOW**

My Photos

Aaargh! I'll never catch Cutie Pie now!

Run, run, as fast as you can! You can't catch Hansel the Gingerbread boy!

Ponies

Saddle up and say howdy to the Ponies, horsey Moshlings with a rich history here in the world of Moshi. Before the invention of the wheel these four-legged little thingummies were often ridden by monsters.

Course, they were far too titchy for big ol' Furis and Katsumas, so as soon as bicycles came along the idea was abandoned. Shame, cos bouncing along on a Magical Mule is great fun — and those ice cream horns of theirs are yummy.

More recently, Ponies were used to pull delivery carts, but you needed a whole bunch of 'em to move anything more than a few Moshimetres. Besides, Princess Ponies thought the whole kit and caboodle was beneath them. Worse still, Silly Snufflers are slower than turtles in peanut butter!

But what about SkyPonies? Well, they were only discovered recently (by yours truly), so nobody knows what they were up to back in the old days. Floating on Cloud Nine, I reckon.

These days Ponies get to do whatever they like in complete freedom — unless I decide to round up a few for my secret ranch. So, quit horsin' around - giddy up and plant a few seeds.

Angel

 # 024

the SkyPony

Personality: dainty, celestial, secretive

Angel

Cloud Nine, high above the Blocky Mountains. I've also spied a few flapping through the Airy Fairy Plains.

Habitat

Until recently, SkyPonies were mentioned only in Moshi legend. But that was before a whole herd appeared, as if by magic, on a pink cloud, high above Mount Sillimanjaro. These heavenly creatures rarely visit ground level, but when they do, they tell tales of a strange world in the sky where everything is soft and fluffy. I wish I could confirm this. Believe me, I've tried. I once leapt on a SkyPony as it was taking off. It didn't take kindly to having a passenger and bucked me off at 39,000ft! Lucky I had my golf brolly to slow down my fall.

Likes: ☺
Playing the harp and maple syrup.

Dislikes: ☹
Saddlebags and drawing pins.

Other Ponies:

	✓
Gigi the Magical Mule	✓
Mr Snoodle the Silly Snuffler	✓
Priscilla the Princess Pony	✓

Code to catch Angel:

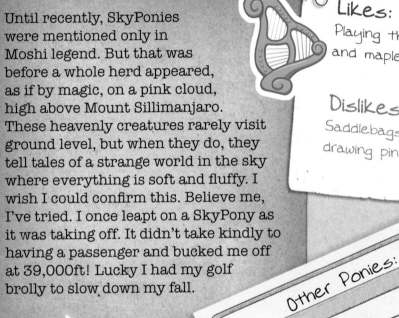

HOT SILLY PEPPERS **ANY** + MAGIC BEANS **ANY** + HOT SILLY PEPPERS **ANY**

Gigi
the Magical Mule

Personality: bewitching, charming, graceful

Gigi

ULTRA RARE

I love fairgrounds!

Likes: ☺
Wild fluttercups and making magical daisy chains.

Dislikes: ☹
The smell of diesel and boiled onions.

Magical Mules are powerful Moshlings descended from enchanted carousel horses. I think that's why they trot along humming fairground tunes, occasionally gliding up and down as if still attached to a merry-go-round. Totally bewitching, these elegant gee-gees love ballroom dancing and can even create rainbows. Shame there's no pot of gold at the end!

When I first tried taming a Magical Mule I could have sworn it was a Lunicorn, but then I grabbed its unihorn and realized it was an ice cream cone held on with liquorice shoelaces. Delicious, and it grows back every time you munch it!

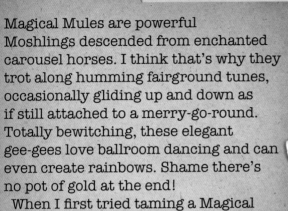

Magical Mules eat cotton candy and wild fluttercups and you can only find those in Crystal Grotto near Copperfield Canyon.

Habitat

Code to catch Gigi:

HOT SILLY PEPPERS **BLUE** + MOON ORCHID **RED** + HOT SILLY PEPPERS **YELLOW**

Mr Snoodle
the Silly Snuffler

056

Personality: slumbersome, dawdly, musical

Zzzzz

Silly Snufflers are the sleepiest, snuffliest Moshlings around – and their sleepiness is contagious. Whenever a monster walks past, it can't help but yawn, stretch and fall asleep on the spot . . . zzzzz. And that's how Silly Snufflers avoid being caught. By the time the monster wakes up, the Snuffler has slowly shuffled away. I've tried every trick in the book to catch one of these snoozy critters. I even snuck up on one after drinking a gallon of black coffee, but I still nodded off, even though my eyelids were propped open with matchsticks. Foiled again!

Likes: ☺ Life in the slow lane and lullabies.

Dislikes: ☹ Giant Goobledegoofs and modern jazz.

Code to catch Mr Snoodle:

HOT SILLY PEPPERS
ANY

+

DRAGON FRUIT
YELLOW

+

HOT SILLY PEPPERS
PURPLE

ZZZZZZ

Sneaking off while
I'm snoozing again...

RARE Mr Snoodle

When they're not shuffling
around, Silly Snufflers graze on
the pumpernickel breadcrumbs of
Franzipan farm, playing ice cream
van melodies with their snouts.

Habitat

ZZZzzz

Priscilla

the Princess Pony

Personality: haughty, fickle, magical

Priscilla

Habitat

Despite their boastful behaviour, I've discovered that Princess Ponies come from a humble area known as Old Knackersville, near Gluey Gulch.

Thought to be descended from royalty, Princess Ponies are always fiddling with their sparkly tiaras, waving their hooves at passers-by and performing pirouettes. If their regal routines fail to impress, prepare to be astounded, because they can make their manes and tails change colour by jingling their jewellery.

One trick ponies? No way! Years ago, I was lucky enough to attend a Princess Pony party. It was a real honour, as I danced with the belle of the ball and was taught how to curtsy like a pony – not easy when you've only got two legs!

Somewhere over the rainbow . . .

Likes: ☺
Sparkly candy apples and winners' rosettes.

Dislikes: ☹
Nosebags (terribly common) and flat shoes.

Code to catch Priscilla:

MOON ORCHID
ANY

+

MOON ORCHID
ANY

+

SNAP APPLE
YELLOW

Where are the Ponies?

Angel

Mr Snoodle

Gigi

Priscilla

Puppies

At first glance these cute little Moshlings seem just like regular doggies - happy and yappy with waggy tails and wet noses. But look a little closer and you'll see they are completely barking.

Yes, they love chewing bones and playing fetch. But they also enjoy dressing up as bouncy-wouncy frogs (Scamp), sipping vintage lemonade (Fifi), sniffing out secrets (McNulty) and tearing rubbish bins to bits (White Fang).

I've even seen a Puppy taking its owner for a walk!

Despite this oddball behaviour (well, they are Moshlings, after all) these mini-mutts make great pets. Just try to keep yours well away from any Kitties, or the fur will fly!

…n yes, and don't be surprised if your
…eds fail to flower when you're trying to
…tract a Puppy. Chances are, one of these
…isky hounds will have dug 'em up and buried
…m in some other monster's backyard.
…ou have been warned. Woof!

Puppies are
barking mad.

Fifi
the Oochie Poochie

Personality: swanky, fashionable, pushy

Fifi

Likes: ☺
Ironed napkins and perfect manners.

Dislikes: ☹
A single hair out of place and being stroked.

Other Puppies:

McNulty the Undercover YapYap	✓
Scamp the Froggie Doggie	✓
White Fang the Musky Husky	✓

Category: Puppies

Ooh la la! Oochie Poochies are sweet, fluffy and totally obsessed with the finer things in life, from fancy food to the very latest fur-styles. In fact, they love getting their fluffy bits trimmed and pampered. Whenever I observe Oochie Poochies they refuse to acknowledge me unless I've trimmed my whiskers and combed my fur. I even have to make an appointment to visit Uppity Meadow!

When they're not sipping vintage lemonade or collecting designer hair clips, these snooty little Moshlings like nibbling on the yummy cotton candy they keep on the end of their tails.

Scrumptious, darling!

Paw print!

Fifi's got it licked!

Oochie Poochies adore the open spaces of Uppity Meadow, but some prefer parading around the Pink and Fluffy Forest.

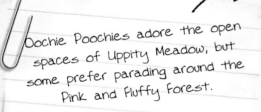

Habitat

Code to catch Fifi:

HOT SILLY PEPPERS **ANY** + DRAGON FRUIT **ANY** + MAGIC BEANS **ANY**

McNulty #038
the Undercover YapYap

Personality:
independent, loyal, furtive

McNulty

Code to catch McNulty:

STAR
BLOSSOM

PURPLE

+

SNAP
APPLE

ANY

+

SNAP
APPLE

ANY

...st ... guess what? Undercover
..pYaps are the nosy puppies
..at love sniffing out secrets,
..mmaging through drawers and
..ing 'psst'. With their plain fur and
..ddlesome looks these cute snoops
..n dupe their way into any situation
..d are also masters of disguise. In
..ct, the only way to be sure you're
..aling with one is to look out for
..at incredibly waggy tail. It's a dead
..veaway! I used to get hoodwinked all
..e time, but not any more. These days
..mploy YapYaps to collect information
.. me. I'm even using my best snoop
.. a top secret mission.

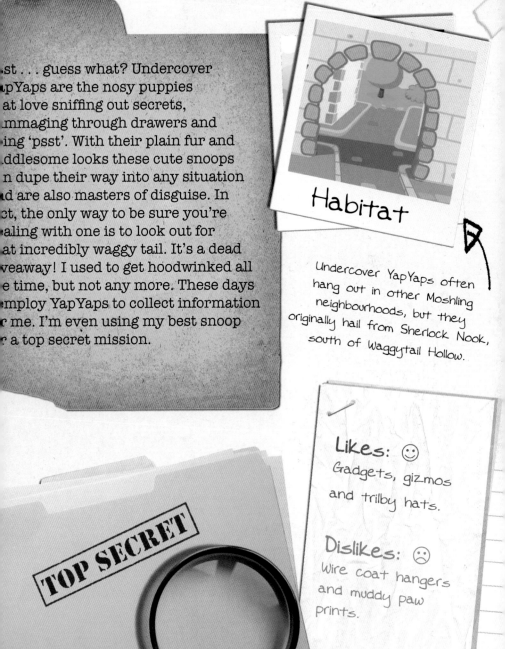

Habitat

Undercover YapYaps often
hang out in other Moshling
neighbourhoods, but they
originally hail from Sherlock Nook,
south of Waggytail Hollow.

Likes: ☺
Gadgets, gizmos
and trilby hats.

Dislikes: ☹
Wire coat hangers
and muddy paw
prints.

TOP SECRET

Scamp

the Froggie Doggie

Personality: loopy-loo, deluded, hilarious

Ribbit!

Ribbit!

Pull here

Ever wondered why a cute little puppy would want to boing around wearing a rubbery frog suit? Me too, but Froggie Doggies are too busy yelling 'ribbit' to answer silly questions. I keep several in my private zoo and I still can't work it out. Maybe there's something in the water? If you know different, feel free to get in touch.

Oh yes, and if you fancy catching one of these jolly pooches, just tug on its pink bow. It deflates that bizarre bouncy outfit in seconds. Ftsssst! If that doesn't work, try popping it with a pin. Bang!

Bang!!!!

Likes: ☺
Pond life and fairy princesses.

Dislikes: ☹
Garlic butter and knitting needles.

Code to catch Scamp:

DRAGON FRUIT		MOON ORCHID		SNAP APPLE
PINK	+	**BLUE**	+	**BLACK**

ULTRA RARE

Ribbit!

Scamp

Habitat

Ribbit!

These dogs think they're frogs, so they often gather at Lillypad Lake and Croak Creek. Bad idea, as they can't swim. Ribbit!

White Fang
the Musky Husky

055

Personality: ravenous, slapdash, wild

Totally barking and slightly whiffy, Musky Huskies are the tail-chasing, bone-loving tearaways that will do almost anything for a bite to eat. I've even seen them rummaging through rubbish bins searching for scraps.

Maybe that's why they always look so scruffy – why groom when you can scoff?

Take care when stroking these greedy pups, or you might lose one of your delicious-looking fingers. Grrrrrr! At the start of a recent expedition a pack of Muskies nabbed my packed lunch. They even chomped my hooting honeybeans and nibbled my hiking stick. Thing is, I was still in my front garden!

Yummy bones!

Likes: ☺
Doggie bags and old bones.

Dislikes: ☹
Detangling lotion and getting tin cans stuck on their noses.

Code to catch White Fang:

MOON ORCHID

RED

+

MAGIC BEANS

RED

+

CRAZY DAISY

ANY

Because they're so hyper, Musky Huskies don't stay put for long. Check out a few skips and you might get lucky.

White Fang age 8 weeks

Habitat

RARE

White Fang

Diary

Well tie me to an anthill and fill my ears with jam! Puppy Moshlings are almost as barking as I am! When they aren't woofing, whiffing, pawing and sniffing, these crazy little canines are usually seeking out monsters to take care of them. And that means they are dog-gone easy to catch, even without seeds or dogfood.

Why, just today I managed to bag myself two Musky Huskies, one Oochie Poochie and seven Froggie Doggies.

Woof woof!

The Huskies were simple. I just followed my nose to the nearest trash can and set a trap consisting of yucky leftovers and a big ol' bucket balanced on a stick. Poo, what a stink! (The Puppies, not the garbage.)

Trapping the Oochie Poochie was more of a challenge. These fancy bow-wows are highly educated, don't you know? I plonked a dinner table in Uppity Meadow and made sure the knives, forks and napkins were all messed up. I knew that any passing Poochies would be unable to resist tidying up — and I was right. The Oochie I nabbed even tried to fold the napkins into swans before my net fell. Oh, I say!

134

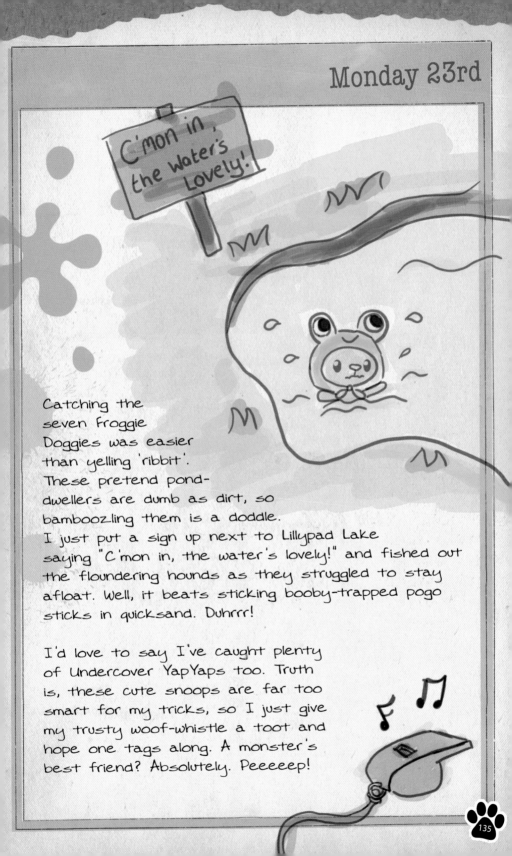

C'mon in, the water's lovely!

Catching the seven Froggie Doggies was easier than yelling 'ribbit'. These pretend pond-dwellers are dumb as dirt, so bamboozling them is a doddle. I just put a sign up next to Lillypad Lake saying "C'mon in, the water's lovely!" and fished out the floundering hounds as they struggled to stay afloat. Well, it beats sticking booby-trapped pogo sticks in quicksand. Duhrrr!

I'd love to say I've caught plenty of Undercover YapYaps too. Truth is, these cute snoops are far too smart for my tricks, so I just give my trusty woof-whistle a toot and hope one tags along. A monster's best friend? Absolutely. Peeeeep!

Kitties

Here kitty, kitty! Say meow to the furry little Moshlings that are amongst the most popular pets in town. In fact, in tests, eight out of ten owners said they preferred collecting Kitties to almost any other Moshling. (The other two were too busy trying to catch Whinger Cats to comment.)

Aside from obvious stuff like paws, claws teeth and tails, Kitties have several other things in common. Most of them enjoy lounging about, having their chins tickled and chasing balls of wool.
They hate hairballs too. Maybe that's w furis often find collecting them a little tricky.

Rare Kitties such as Tabby Nerdicats are hard to entice, as they seldom leave home and find Moshling flowers a little boring. Actually, come to think of it, all four Kitties seem to prefer home comforts to the great outdoors.

This is probably because they want to avoid bumping into any Puppies. They're scared stiff of the yappy little pooches! In fact, the only time I've ever seen a Kitty scarper was when a Tubby Huggishi came face to face with a Musky Husky. It dashed back home to OuchiPoo Park before you could say

"Purrrrr."

Gingersnap
the Whinger Cat   # 003

Personality: sluggish, cantankerous, cynical

Gingersnap

Other Kitties:

Lady Meowford the Pretty Kitty

Purdy the Tubby Huggishi

Waldo the Tabby Nerdicat

Why is Gingersnap so whingy? ... always in a bad mewd!

Grand gateau, yummy!

Paw Prints

Moany, lazy, but strangely charming, Whinger Cats are said to be really good at fixing stuff. I'm not sure this is true, because they never bother showing up, even when I've ordered pizza for everyone. Maybe it's because they're busy waiting for other things – like bedtime and dinnertime. The first time I encountered one I mistook it for a cushion and sat on it. It didn't even flinch.
  If you come across a Whinger don't expect it to move unless you've got a big handful of melted cheese – food is almost as important as sleep to these lovable layabouts. Yawn!

Likes: ☺
All-inclusive hotels and melted anything.

Dislikes: ☹
Work, work and work.

Habitat

Whinger Cats are rarely seen outside as they spend most of their time chillaxing by Sloth Swamp near Hopeless Hill.

Code to catch Gingersnap:

HOT SILLY PEPPERS — ANY

+

LOVE BERRIES — ANY

+

MAGIC BEANS — ANY

Lady Meowford

the Pretty Kitty

 # 030

Personality: snippy, sophisticated, snooty

Lady Meowford

Code to catch Lady Meowford:

STAR BLOSSOM
ANY

+

MOON ORCHID
ANY

+

MOON ORCHID
BLUE

harp

Frightfully sweet but a bit annoying, these cute Moshlings are always right about everything. Well okay, there was one time when a Pretty Kitty thought it was wrong, but it turned out to be right all along. Snooty but impossibly charming, Pretties are very musical and have incredibly high-pitched singing voices. They also speak several languages, are very good skiers, fabulous lacrosse players and know everything about everything. I usually have to wear a tie and dinner jacket to get anywhere near one, and even then I can only speak when spoken to.

Likes: ☺
Classical music and toffee-nosed plums.

Dislikes: ☹
Balls of string and kebabs.

Habitat

Pretty Kitties live way up in the High and Mighty Mountains. Everywhere else is beneath them.

Purdy
the Tubby Huggishi

Personality: greedy, catty, lardy

Habitat

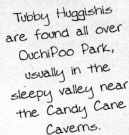

Tubby Huggishis are found all over OuchiPoo Park, usually in the sleepy valley near the Candy Cane Caverns.

Tubby Huggishis are highly huggable Moshlings that spend most days preening themselves and lounging about eating piles of pastry. That's why most of them are a little on the large side – good news for me as it makes 'em mighty easy to snag and tag. I've even had one eating fairy cakes from my hand. Big mistake as it darn near chewed my fingers clean off!

When they're not scoffing cakes, these shaggy felines enjoy giving advice to other Moshlings, dipping their paws in syrup and meowing to their friends about the price of lard.

Code to catch Purdy:

DRAGON FRUIT **ANY** + MOON ORCHID **ANY** + DRAGON FRUIT **ANY**

Purdy

Likes: 🙂
Drinking condensed
milk and licking
stamps.

Dislikes: ☹️
Water pistols
and salad.

Waldo

the Tabby Nerdicat

Personality: dweebish, tech-savvy, inventive

Waldo

RARE

Code to catch Waldo:

DRAGON FRUIT

ANY

+

LOVE BERRIES

PINK

+

STAR BLOSSOM

RED

I thought I was geeky, but Tabby Nerdicats can tell you the square root of a banana faster than you can say "sci-fi convention". I even managed to persuade one to repair my camera after I dropped it in the bath – it makes the tea now, as well as taking photos!

Nerdis spend most days (and nights) fiddling with circuit boards, arguing over comics and listening to Quantum Physics Hour on Fangdoodle FM. Trying to find one is harder than reverse algebra, but I've discovered they like toffee nachos.

Never ask 'em to dance. They can't.

Habitat

These studious Moshlings spend most of their time in cubbyholes by the grassy knoll on Honeycomb Hill. Do not disturb!

Likes: ☺
Untangling pretzels and fixing soldering irons.

Dislikes: ☹
Good dancers and contact lenses.

My Photos

Here, kitty, kitty, kitty . . .

Cheese is always the answer when Gingersnap's part of the equation.

Spookies

Woo-ooh! You can come out from behind the sofa — Spookies aren't that scary. Okay, these supernatural Moshlings can be a little creepy, but most of them are pretty friendly. Well, kind of.

I must admit I didn't believe in ghosts - let alone little Banshees, Hoodoos and Heebees — till I spotted something drifting past my tent one stormy night during an expedition to Fang-Ten Valley.

Turns out it was one of them there pesky Squidge critters trying to drain ol' Buster dry. Lucky I sleep with my scarf on and my tent zipped - no bloodsucker's getting its teeth into this here juicy neck!

Since then I've learnt everything there is to know about Spookies. These mysterious Moshlings can plop out of plasma clouds, drift through walls, cast spells, turn you inside out and give even the bravest of collectors the willies.

But not me, oh no. Thanks to my nerves of steel I've caught ghosties galore and . . . Aargh! What was that? Oh, it's just my jimmy jams flapping on the clothes line. Where was I? Oh yes, on the following pages I'll tell you what seeds you need to start collecting Spookies. So don't be a scaredy-cat, get huntin'.

Mwah-ha-ha!

Big Bad Bill # 089

the Woolly Blue Hoodoo

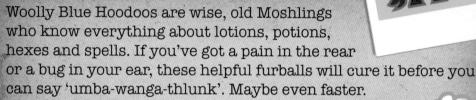

Personality: wise, mystical, generous

Woolly Blue Hoodoos are wise, old Moshlings who know everything about lotions, potions, hexes and spells. If you've got a pain in the rear or a bug in your ear, these helpful furballs will cure it before you can say 'umba-wanga-thlunk'. Maybe even faster.

I once got bitten by a ten metre skeeter during a trip to the Barmy Swami Jungle. A Hoodoo saved my life by kissing it better (the skeeter, not my bite). Phew! Never seen without their mystical Staffs of Power, Woolly Blue Hoodoos are really scared of teaspoons. Maybe they don't like their own medicine.

Habitat

Naturally nomadic, Woolly Blue Hoodoos wander vast areas in search of enlightenment and bald peaches. According to my great uncle's notes, they come from a lost tribe found deep in the Gombala Gombala Jungle.

Likes: ☺
Deep massage and deep-fried Oobla Doobla.

Dislikes: ☹
Clowns and itchy eyeballs.

ULTRA RARE

Big Bad Bill

Code to catch Big Bad Bill:

STAR BLOSSOM **BLUE** + LOVE BERRIES **YELLOW** + STAR BLOSSOM **BLACK**

Ecto
the Fancy Banshee

Personality: ephemeral, spooky, silent

RARE

Ecto

WOO-OO-OO

Habitat

Scientists can scoff, but I think Fancy Banshees come from a parallel vortex deep within the ClothEar Cloud formation. It can only be accessed by running around shouting "woo-oo-oo" really loudly.

Psst . . . don't be afraid, Fancy Banshees are quite friendly. Just make sure you don't touch one, because their shimmering capes are made of electrified wobble-plasma, mysterious stuff that turns things inside-out. How do I know? Yep, you guessed it, I got Ectoed! It happened when I was exploring Collywobbles Castle. I never did find my compass. Or my back teeth.

When they're not drifting through walls in the dead of night, these totally silent Moshlings float around collecting Rox dust. No one knows why, but I believe they need to absorb it to keep glowing.

Likes: 😊
Rox dust and darkness.

Dislikes: ☹
Anyone called Ichabod and being upside-down.

What's Ecto's favourite fruit? Booberries!

Code to catch Ecto:

HOT SILLY PEPPERS ANY

+

LOVE BERRIES RED

+

LOVE BERRIES BLACK

Kissy
the Baby Ghost

Personality: cute, frangible, shy

Kissy

Kissy's favourite bedtime story is *Ghouldilocks and the Three Scares.*

These charming Moshlings plop out of the plasma clouds high above the abandoned Harem Scarum pickling plant in the Okay-ish Lands.

Habitat

t's hard being scary when you're as cute as a Baby Ghost. These supernatural Moshlings are more interested in tutus, oys, false eyelashes nd pink ribbons than sneaking round frightening Moshi Monsters. I even kept a couple as pets years ago, ut they kept arguing over who got he fluffy cushion in my tent (and us collectors needs plenty of shut-eye). If you do see a Baby Ghost, try ot to breathe near it, or it might evaporate, leaving just a bow and pair of soggy pink pumps. I think hat's what happened to mine. Oops!

Likes: ☺
Fluffy poodles and loganberry lip gloss.

Dislikes: ☹
Suction cups and sponges.

Code to catch Kissy:

STAR BLOSSOM

ANY

+

MAGIC BEANS

ANY

+

STAR BLOSSOM

PURPLE

Squidge

the Furry Heebee

onality: diabolical, creepy, bitey-witey

Squidge

Code to catch Squidge:

 +  +

HOT SILLY PEPPERS	STAR BLOSSOM	DRAGON FRUIT
ANY	ANY	ANY

It's rare to see a Furry Heebee at all, but if you do it will be hanging upside-down in the Crazy Caves of Fang-Ten Valley.

Habitat

Super-cute? Not really. A Furry Heebee's bite is worse than its bark. That's because these flying Moshlings are greedy bloodsuckers that flutter around after dark hunting for juicy victims. I never go looking for them without my splat-tastic swatter, and I always wear a polo neck jumper. When they can't find any necks to nip, Heebee's will settle for a nice mug of instant tomato soup with plenty of garlicky croutons – and that's how I catch 'em. Oh yes, about the bark: it's more of a high-pitched "mwah-ha-ha", but it's still enough to give you goosebumps!

Likes: ☺
Long capes and scary organ music.

Dislikes: ☹
Heebee-repellent spray and figures-of-eight.

Where are the Spookies?

Squidge

Kissy

Ecto

Big Bad Bill

Slug Punzel
The Slug Princess

#55

Personality: Grmpy, Aragant, ugly

Of course, new Moshlings come
along all the time, so record yc
own sightings on these pages.
But don't forget to share the
news with your collecting chums!

Habitat

Top Secret

Likes: ☺
mirror's
big
houes

Dislikes: ☹
Broken
mirror is
Loud singing

Code to catch my Moshling:

Star Storm + Snap apple + Puffin

My Moshling

Rosyretta

#

Personality: moody

Habitat

Likes: ☺

Dislikes: ☹

Category: FLOLERS

Code to catch my Moshling:

+ +

My Moshling

Personality:

#

Code to catch my Moshling:

+ +

Category:

Habitat

Likes: ☺

Dislikes: ☹

\#

Personality:

Habitat

Likes: ☺

Dislikes: ☹

Category:

Code to catch my Moshling:

+ +

............**'s**

Big Bad Bill
#89

Ultra rare!

Ecto
#60

Kissy
#27

Squidge
#08

DJJQuack
#13

Prof.Purplex
#74

Tiki
#65

Peppy
#71

Waldo
#77

Gingersnap
#03

Lady Meowford
#30

Purdy
#20

Coolio
#52

Ultra rare!

Cutie Pie
#91

Ultra rare!

Oddie
#88

Hansel
#59

Sooki-Yaki
#47

Chop Chop
#02

Ultra rare!

General Fuzuki
#82

Shelby
#39

Liberty
#61

Ultra rare!

Cleo
#80

Rocky
#28

Ultra rare!

Mini Ben
#97

MOSHLING ZOO

Priscilla
#48

Gigi
#79
Ultra rare!

Mr.Snoodle
#56

Angel
#24

Cali
#72

Fumble
#53

Stanley
#18

Blurp
#43

Doris
#40

Pooky
#50

Gurgle
#83
Ultra rare!

Snookums
#10

ShiShi
#87

Jeepers
#73

Burnie
#78
Ultra rare!

Humphrey
#23

Honey
#57

Dipsy
#34

Flumpy
#54

IGGY
#100
Ultra rare!

Fifi
#07

McNulty
#38

Scamp
#84
Ultra rare!

White Fang
#55

The Daily

CAPTURED!

Breaking news! New Moshling, Roxy the Precious Prism, has finally been caught by Moshling Collector Extraordinaire, Buster Bumblechops!

Bumblechops said, "I've been seeking that sparkly little lady for months, but she always managed to slip out of my grasp. Not this time though!" Buster told *The Daily Growl* that he'd been digging up mutant sprouts in his allotment when a glistening glint in the distance caught his eye. He refused to reveal the exact location as he's hoping that more mystery Moshlings might be attracted to the hidden hangout in the near future . . .

Above: Roxy at 2:00pm

New Games!

Our roving reporter has heard that exciting new games are always available in Monstro City! Pop into the Moshi Fun Park and test your skills now!

Above: Mystery Mo

Above: Moshi Fun Park

Growl

Get your own Roxy!

Catching Roxy shouldn't be so tricky for the rest of us! Buster Bumblechops is willing to share his secret with readers of *The Daily Growl* and help all Official Moshling Collectors to get their hands on this priceless prize. Simply email Buster at **buster@moshimonsters.com** to find out more . . .

Inside today's *Daily Growl*:

- MonSTAR of the week!
- Room of the week!
- Agony Ant's fortunes!
- Shout Outs!

ore Mystery Moshlings

mours abound t Roxy is not the ly new Moshling have been spotted ound Monstro ity! Three other Mystery Moshlings have been spotted, but no clear pictures have been taken as yet. Keep an eye out for them though, and let us know if you find them!

Rox Lottery

Latest random Rox winners announced inside! Check out page 32 to see if you're one of our big winners!

Roxy
the Precious Prism

101

Personality: priceless, fastidious, fragile

Roxy

SECRET

You've got to be quick to catch Roxy!

How to catch Roxy:
This sparkling secret Moshling can only be caught by the most clued-up collectors. Email buster@moshimonsters.com to find out how to add her to your collection!

Deep beneath the Twinkly-Dink mines of Kaleido Island lays a rich seam of powerful Rox. But Precious Prisms don't hang out down there. It's far too obvious! Plus they might bump into ol' Buster diggin' for sparkly stuff. These secret Moshlings are so priceless they're scared to lay a finger on anything (including themselves!) in case they leave smudges. That's why they wear silly white gloves 24/7. But so would you, if you were made of 100% pure Rox. The only way to catch 'em is to get diggin'. Handle with care; they often shatter into squillions of pieces.

Zzing!

Sparkling in the sunshine

Likes: ☺
Vinegar baths and buffing machines.

Dislikes: ☹
Magpies and fingerprints.

I once spotted a Priceless Prism during the Great Rox Rush of Eleventy Seven, but I can't remember where.

Drat!

My work here is done . . .
until the next Moshling comes along . . .